A LIFE OF CHRIST

HARPER JUBILEE BOOKS

A LIFE OF CHRIST

Text by WILLIAM BARCLAY

Scripted by Iain Reid · Cartoons by Eric Fraser

HARPER & ROW, PUBLISHERS
New York, Hagerstown, San Francisco, London

FIRST EDITION

ISBN: 0–06–060403–4

LIBRARY OF CONGRESS CATALOG CARD NUMBER: 76–9989

A HARPER JUBILEE GIANT ORIGINAL

CONTENTS

1

MARY EXPECTS JESUS

The most notable thing about the Jews is that they never lost hope that one day the Messiah would come and would lead them to the position in the world which they believed was their due. Messiah and Christ are the same word. They both mean 'anointed', and the Messiah was the anointed being whom God was going to send into the world to vindicate the Jesus and to bring in an earthly kingdom.

When Mary was about to marry Joseph she discovered that she was pregnant. Matthew and Luke tell the story of what is known as the Virgin Birth. That is the story which tells that Jesus was born into the world without the help of any human father. But, strange to say, when Matthew and Luke give the genealogy of Jesus they trace that genealogy through Joseph, which would be meaningless if Joseph was not his earthly father. So we may take it that in this story there is a double tradition. There is the tradition of the Virgin Birth, that Jesus was born of no earthly father but of the Holy Spirit. But there is also the tradition that Jesus was born as the child of Joseph but that in his birth the Holy Spirit was operative as never before or since. The Jews had a saying: 'In the birth of any child there are three partners, the father, the mother and the Holy One, blessed be He.' The Jews believed that no child was born without the intervention of God, and this story at all events stresses that God specially intervened in the birth of Jesus.

Although the Jews had been a subject nation for 700 years and more, they never lost their faith that God would keep his promises to them...

They believed that a Messiah would arise from the line of David who would throw their conquerors out of Palestine and lead the Jews to world conquest

1

JOSEPH, YOU ARE A DESCENDANT OF DAVID, AREN'T YOU?

YES, I AM, MARY

WHAT IF I WERE TO HAVE A BABY, AND THIS BABY TURNED OUT TO BE THE MESSIAH?

THAT WOULD INDEED BE WONDERFUL!

WELL, JOSEPH, I *AM* GOING TO HAVE A BABY, AND I BELIEVE THAT THE BABY IS GOING TO BE THE PERSON THROUGH WHOM GOD WILL KEEP HIS PROMISES

The Jews had a saying that, in the birth of any child, there were *THREE* partners— the father, the mother and the Holy one, blessed be he

GOD BE PRAISED!

There was going to be a birth in Palestine in which God, the Holy one, was operative as he had never been in any other birth in history

2

JESUS IN THE TEMPLE

In Palestine among the Jews a boy became a man when he was twelve years old. He became a Bar Mitzvah, which means a Son of the Commandment. When the boy was twelve, he had to take upon himself the duty of obeying the Law like any adult person. One of the regulations in the Law was that anyone who stayed within fifteen miles of Jerusalem must attend the Passover. So when Jesus was twelve he was taken to his first Passover Feast, the feast that commemorated the deliverance of the Jews from Egypt. At the end of the feast he lingered on in Jerusalem. His parents did not miss him because the women and the men travelled in separate companies. The women, because they travelled more slowly, set out in advance of the men and the two companies met at the first night's stopping place. Joseph had thought that Jesus was with Mary, and Mary had thought that Jesus was with Joseph, and so they did not miss him until the first night's stopping place was reached.

When he was not there, they retraced their steps to Jerusalem and they found Jesus there. During the Passover time the Sanhedrin, the supreme council of the Jews, held its discussions in public and they found Jesus there, hearing them and asking them questions. This does not mean that he was, as it were, taking charge. It is the normal phrase for a pupil learning.

The important thing is what Jesus said. Mary said to him: 'Did you not know that your father and I sought you and were desperately worried?' Note Jesus' answer. Very gently he takes the word 'Father' from Joseph and gives it to God. 'Did you not know that I would be in my father's house?' This was surely the beginning of Jesus' realisation of his special relationship to God.

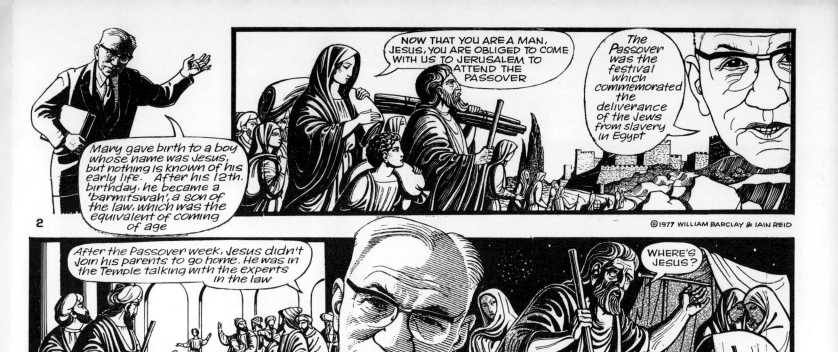

Mary gave birth to a boy whose name was Jesus, but nothing is known of his early life. After his 12th. birthday, he became a 'barmitswah', a son of the law, which was the equivalent of coming of age

NOW THAT YOU ARE A MAN, JESUS, YOU ARE OBLIGED TO COME WITH US TO JERUSALEM TO ATTEND THE PASSOVER

The Passover was the festival which commemorated the deliverance of the Jews from slavery in Egypt

2

After the Passover week, Jesus didn't join his parents to go home. He was in the Temple talking with the experts in the law

WHERE'S JESUS?

I NEVER MET A LAD WHO SEEMED TO KNOW SO MUCH ABOUT GOD

Meanwhile, Mary and Joseph arrived separately at the first night's camping ground, the women having set out ahead of the men because they travelled more slowly

I THOUGHT HE WOULD BE WITH YOU, JOSEPH, NOW THAT HE IS A MAN

AND I THOUGHT HE WAS WITH YOU, MARY! IF WE DON'T FIND HIM HERE, WE MUST RETURN TO JERUSALEM

JESUS! HOW COULD YOU DO THIS TO US? YOUR FATHER AND I HAVE BEEN SEARCHING FOR YOU FOR THREE DAYS!

DIDN'T YOU KNOW I WAS BOUND TO BE IN MY FATHER'S HOUSE?

From that time, Jesus was aware that, in a unique sense, God was his father, and he was God's son

3

JESUS
DECIDES TO
SEE JOHN

When Jesus was thirty events happened which stirred all Jerusalem. John the Baptist emerged and was baptising people in the Jordan for the repentance and remission of their sins. Jesus decided to go and be baptised by John. It is natural to wonder why. If Jesus was sinless, he had no sins to repent of and to be baptised for, but Jesus went because there was amongst the people a great movement of repentance at that time. They came out in their hundreds to be baptised by John, and Jesus felt that he must identify himself with a nation seeking God. He felt that in that search for God, for him the hour had struck.

Jesus was now aware that, in a unique sense, he was God's son, and God was his father. But the figure who at that time filled the horizon was John who was calling upon the Jews to come to Jordan

REPENT OF YOUR SINS AND COME AND BE WASHED

3

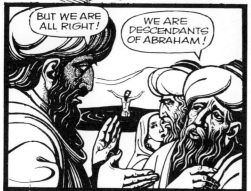

BUT WE ARE ALL RIGHT!

WE ARE DESCENDANTS OF ABRAHAM!

IT IS NOT YOUR DESCENT, BUT YOUR **DEEDS** THAT MATTER

© 1977 WILLIAM BARCLAY & IAIN REID

JESUS, HAVE YOU HEARD WHAT YOUR COUSIN JOHN IS DOING?

I HAVE, MOTHER

John was calling upon the Jews to be baptised. No Jew had ever been baptised before. They thought they didn't need to be. There was now a consciousness of sin such as the Jews had never had before

I HAVE A STRANGE FEELING, MOTHER, THAT I MUST GO AND BE BAPTISED BY JOHN

Jesus was not himself a sinner, but he was convinced that he must now identify himself with men's search for God

4

THE BAPTISM

When the people came to John to be baptised, he asked them, 'Who has warned you to flee from the wrath to come?' He saw them in terms of a desert picture. The desert was covered with stubble and brushwood as dry as tinder. Sometimes that brushwood and those bushes caught fire, and as the fire swept through it you could see small animals racing in front of the fire to escape, and John likens the people who came to be baptised to those animals seeking to escape the desert fire.

When Jesus was baptised, a voice came to him: 'You are my son, the beloved and only one, in whom I am well pleased'. This is surely the second great step in Jesus' realisation of his personality and his task. It is the voice of God telling him that the time has come for him to go out and preach and speak to men.

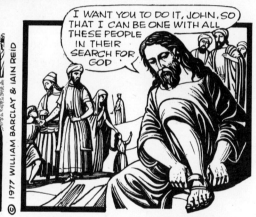

5

THE WILDERNESS

When Jesus had heard God's voice at the baptism he knew the time had come for him to go out and to preach publicly to the people, but before he set out he had to decide just exactly what he was going to do and how he was going to do it. The Jews had their dream of a Messiah all right, but for the most part their dream was of a conquering Messiah who would lead their armies to triumph over the world. Their Messiah was a material Messiah. In the desert Jesus had his temptations. We must not think of one temptation coming and leaving, then a second coming and leaving him and a third coming and leaving him. We must think of the whole matter going on in Jesus' mind for the forty days he was there.

His first temptation was to turn the stones of the desert into bread. They were exactly like little round loaves. But his answer is that man needs more than bread to live, he needs the voice of God. His second temptation was to jump down from the Temple pinnacle and flutter down and land unharmed in the Temple Court, thereby giving men a sensation such as they had never seen before, but he decides that is not the way, because that would be trying to see how far you could go with God. The third temptation was to bow down and worship Satan. This is the temptation to compromise, not to set his standards quite so high and come to a working arrangement with evil, but Jesus says no, right is right and wrong is wrong and they are for ever and eternally different.

So in the desert Jesus makes up his mind what his message is to be. He has to work not as the conquering hero. He has to work as the suffering Messiah, whose kingdom comes through suffering and not through might.

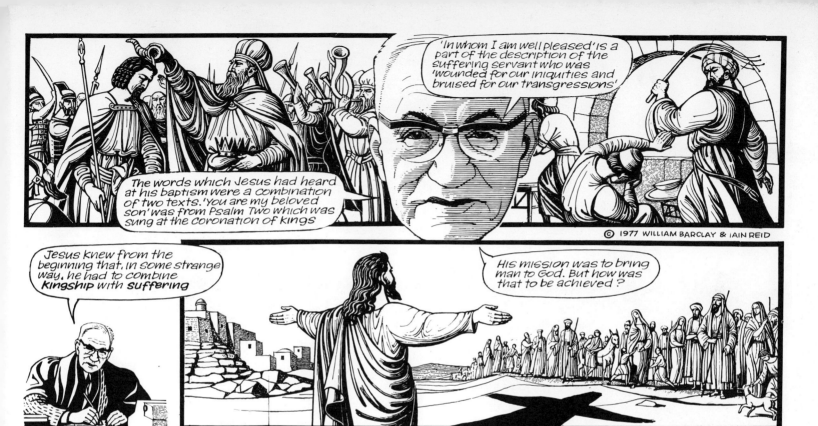

The words which Jesus had heard at his baptism were a combination of two texts. 'You are my beloved son' was from Psalm Two which was sung at the coronation of kings

'In whom I am well pleased' is a part of the description of the suffering servant who was 'wounded for our iniquities and bruised for our transgressions'

Jesus knew from the beginning that, in some strange way, he had to combine **kingship** with **suffering**

His mission was to bring man to God. But how was that to be achieved?

He went out to the desert to plan his campaign. He was conscious of special powers, and the temptation to be the traditional Messiah was very strong

His battle with temptation was to last forty days and forty nights

5

6

THE TEMPTATIONS

This story has a special quality because if there is any truth in it—and we believe there is—it can have only one source. It must have come from Jesus himself, because during the experience of the temptations he was alone.

The temptations story is the story of events taking place in Jesus' mind. This is easily seen in Matthew in the third temptation, where the tempter takes Jesus up into a high mountain and shows him all the kingdoms of the world. Of course there is no such mountain in the world from which all the world's kingdoms may be seen. This is a mental picture which is being described. In another way to think of the temptations, we think of them happening, as it were, one after another. We are not to think of three separate acts of temptation, we are to think of forty days and nights when Jesus fought his continual struggle with the tempter.

The point of the temptations is Jesus deciding what method he will use to do his work. He will not use the method of offering the people bread. He will not use the method of cheap sensations. He will not use the method of a compromise with evil. He will take the way of utter obedience to God, no matter what the cost.

We note finally that Luke says that the devil left him until another opportune time came. The temptations of Jesus were continuous. It is to be noted that twice the tempter began his temptation by saying: 'If you are the Son of God . . .' (Matthew 3.3–6). The tempter was trying to make Jesus doubt his own destiny and his own self, and it came at the end again, because in Matthew 27.40 the crowds shout to Jesus: 'If you are the Son of God, come down from the cross'. If Jesus had begun to doubt his own destiny, his action would have been completely paralysed. We therefore see Jesus realising his destiny and settling his method of attaining it.

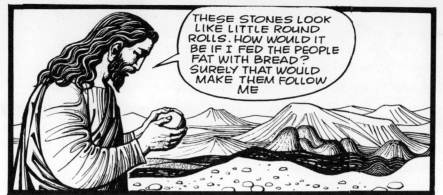

6

7

THE MESSAGE

We have seen Jesus know that his hour had come. We have seen him assured by God that this was indeed the case. We have seen him join himself to the national movement in search of God. We have seen him settle what method he was going to use in his crusade and now we have to look at his message. His message was, the time is fulfilled and the kingdom of God is at hand; repent and believe in the gospel. His message was, the kingdom of Heaven is just about to come. The word 'kingdom' in this context does not mean an area of land, as we might speak about the United Kingdom. The word 'kingdom' is really the word 'kingship'. The kingship of God is about to come, or, as we might put it in more modern language, God is about to begin his reign.

What is the kingdom of God? When we come to the Lord's Prayer (Matthew 6.10) we find Jesus teaching men to pray: 'Thy Kingdom come, Thy will be done in earth as it is in Heaven'. Hebrew writers had a way of saying everything twice and dividing it in the middle, so that the second half of what they said implied or explained the first half. Any verse of the Psalms will show this happening. For instance, 'God is our refuge and strength'. Then the second half 'A very present help in trouble', which explains or implies the first half. If we take it that the two phrases in the Lord's Prayer are written like this, if we take it that the second half explains the first half, then we get a definition, the kingdom of God or the kingdom of Heaven is a society on earth in which God's will is as perfectly done as it is in Heaven.

This is to say that whenever we do God's will we are in the kingdom. So far, this is only spasmodically true. The kingdom of God is a time when all men shall know and obey God.

Jesus had to decide his message to mankind. He chose something simple, something familiar to the Jews...

THE KINGDOM OF GOD IS AT HAND... REPENT AND BELIEVE IN GOD

In Greek, the word is not "kingdom", but "kingship", and this is what Jesus meant, not a **place** but the reign of God in men's hearts

ΒΑΣΙΛΕΙΑ

The Lord's Prayer makes this clear when it is remembered that the Jews always repeated everything for emphasis and amplification

THY KINGDOM COME ... THY WILL BE DONE, ON EARTH AS IT IS IN HEAVEN

If we assume that the second part explains the first part, the Kingdom of God is defined as the society on earth in which God's will is done as it is in Heaven

© 1977 WILLIAM BARCLAY & IAIN REID

For Jesus, the most important thing is to do the will of God. **That** is the kingdom!

The second part of his message is then quite clear. "Repent" means to turn and face the other way. He was telling the Jews to stop thinking of their might, majesty and power, and to start thinking about **God**

This was hard for the Jews to accept, believing as they did that the Kingdom of God will mark God's breaking into history with a show of strength to establish them as masters of the world

7

8

CALLING THE DISCIPLES

There are three accounts of Jesus calling his disciples. In Mark 3.14 it is said that he called them to be with him and to be sent out. They were called to be with him, that is to say, he needed their friendship and their companionship. They were called to be sent out. The companionship of Jesus fitted them to be sent out on his work. The second is in Luke. In Luke 6.13 we are told that Jesus called twelve men out of the general body of his disciples and Luke says he called these twelve men apostles. The word 'apostle' is a Greek word which literally means 'one who is sent out' and it can also mean an ambassador. So the disciples were chosen to be the ambassadors of Jesus Christ. The third account is in Matthew 10.1 and 5, where we are told that Jesus called his disciples and gave them power to do the same kind of things as he did and then sent them out. In Matthew you could say that the apostles were Jesus' delegates. He delegated some of his power to them.

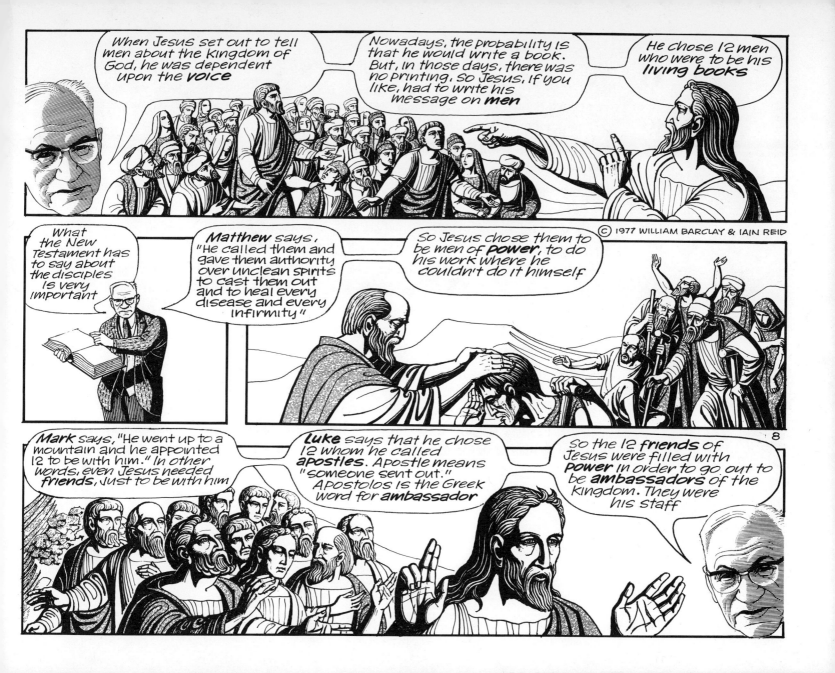

9

MATTHEW

Matthew was a tax gatherer, and that is to say he belonged to a class of people who were the best-hated people in Palestine. Palestine at the moment was subject to the Romans. The Romans did not themselves collect taxes. They sold the right to collect taxes in a given area to the highest bidder. The people did not know what they had to pay because there was no way of making a general announcement of it, and whatever the tax collector could extract over and above the sum he had contracted for he was allowed to keep. So those who became tax collectors were regarded as traitors to their country and to their fellow Jews because they collected taxes for the Romans. There were different kinds of taxes. There were the stated taxes. Stated taxes were one-tenth of a man's corn and grapes and olives, partly in kind and partly in money. One percent of income was income tax, and thirdly, every Jew from fourteen to sixty-five had to pay a poll tax simply for the privilege of living in the empire. These taxes were not so serious because people did know what they had to pay. The kind of taxes in which the tax collector really made his cut were what we would call customs duties. There was a tax to use a main road or a harbour. There was tax on a cart, a tax on each wheel and a tax on the animal who pulled it. There was import and export duty and frequently a tax collector would stop a merchant on the road, tell him to open his bundles, and there and then extract this, that and the next tax on what the merchant was carrying. So rare was a good tax collector that a Roman historian said as a joke that he once saw a monument to an honest tax collector. This is what Matthew was. Matthew would be despised and hated by his fellow Jews, but Jesus saw in him material to make an apostle.

9

10

ANDREW

There is something very attractive about Andrew.

1. He was the first disciple to be called (John 1.35–42; Mark 1.16,17).

2. He is always described as Peter's brother, as if he were not important enough to stand on his own feet. Having been the first called he might well have expected the first place, but he handed that over to his brother and apparently felt no envy, no jealousy and no discontent.

3. Every time we hear of Andrew he is bringing someone to Jesus. He begins by bringing his brother Peter (John 1.41). Secondly, he brings the boy with the five loaves and the two small fishes with which Jesus fed the multitude (John 6.8 and 9), and thirdly, he brings to Jesus the Greeks who had come to Philip saying: 'Sir, we would see Jesus' (John 12.20–23). Wherever Andrew appears he appears as bringing someone to Jesus.

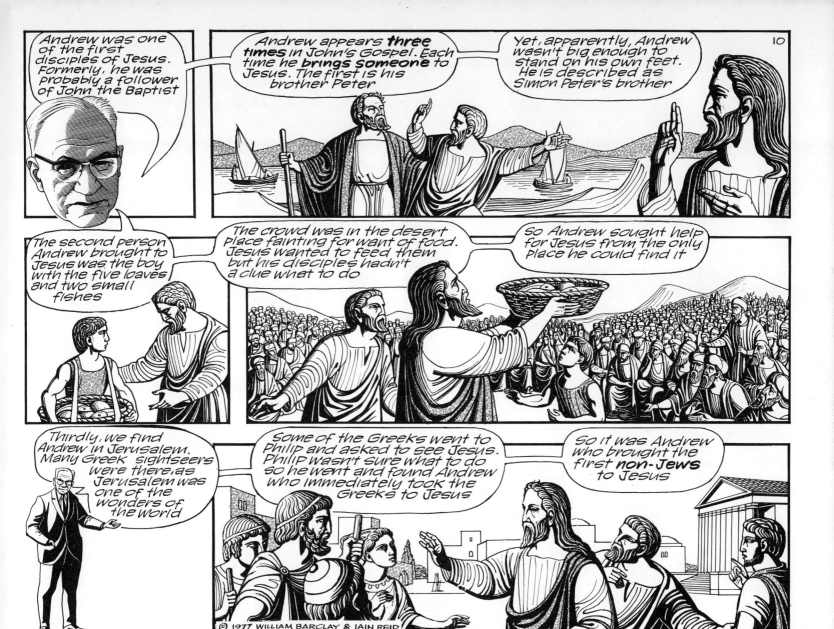

11

PETER

The Gospel of Mark has two great events in Peter's life. First, he was the disciple who was the first to realise who Jesus really was (Mark 8.27–30) and that was a great thing. Secondly, he was the disciple who denied Jesus when Jesus was on trial and who refused to have any connection with him whatsoever (Mark 14.66–72). It is generally held that Mark's Gospel consists of the preaching material of Peter and of Peter's memories. He was not able to write Greek himself and he got Mark to write it for him. It is very surprising that in what is his own Gospel he gives so much space to his denial of Jesus. It is as if Peter were saying: 'Look what I did, and look how he still trusted me'.

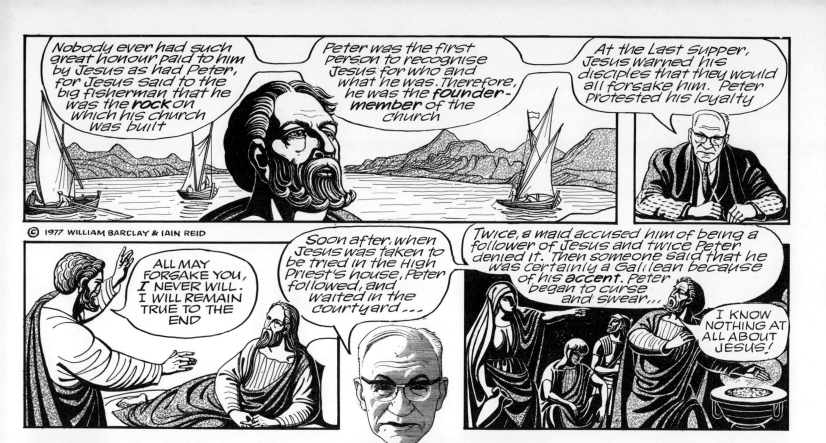

11

12

THOMAS

Thomas will always be regarded as doubting Thomas. There are two outstanding moments in Thomas's life. The first was when word came to Jesus and his disciples that Lazarus was ill and that Lazarus had died. When Jesus heard this he decided that he would go to Bethany, which was a very short distance from Jerusalem, to see if he could help. The disciples were worried about this because they knew very well that to go to Bethany, so close to Jerusalem, was for Jesus to put his head into the lion's den, and perhaps there was some doubt if they would follow him at all, when suddenly the normally silent Thomas said quietly, 'Let us go also that we may die with him'. Thomas may have been a pessimist but he was a brave pessimist. The second important moment in Thomas's life is told in John 20.19–29. When Jesus appeared first of all to the ten disciples Thomas was not there and he would not believe that Jesus had risen from the dead. This was far too good to be true. Jesus came back again and this time Thomas was there. Thomas said that he would not believe unless Jesus let him thrust his hand into the wound in his side and put his finger into the print of the nails. Jesus offered to let Thomas do this, but Thomas believed with the words 'My Lord and my God'. It took Thomas a long time to make up his mind, but when he did make up his mind, he was settled.

© 1977 WILLIAM BARCLAY & IAIN REID

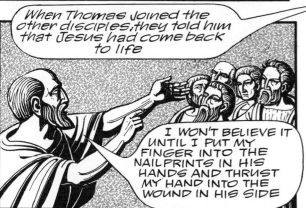

13

JUDAS

Everyone must wonder why Judas betrayed Jesus. Various answers have been given.

1. He is Judas Iscariot. Iscariot could be *ish kerioth,* which would mean 'man of Kerioth.' If Judas was a man of Kerioth, he was the only non-Galilean in the apostolic band. He was the one lowlander amonst eleven highlanders, and he may have been neglected from the beginning.

2. It is suggested that Judas turned king's evidence, that when he saw the ship was sinking he got out. If he did, he made the most dreadful bargain in history, because he betrayed Jesus for the normal price of a slave.

3. Judas may have been a violent nationalist. Iscariot may be the Greek form of the Latin word *sicarius,* and *sicarius* means 'dagger bearer'. The dagger bearers were violent nationalists who were pledged to the assassination of every Roman they could get their hands on, and it may be that Judas saw in Jesus the very leader the nationalists needed and joined him, and then when he saw that Jesus was going to walk the way of love and not of power, he turned against him and betrayed him.

4. It is probable that the fourth idea of Judas is the right one. It starts the same way as the third with Judas the nationalist trying to ally himself with Jesus and being disappointed. This theory goes on to say that when that happened Judas betrayed Jesus not with any intention that Jesus should be killed, but with the intention of putting Jesus into a position in which he would have to act for his own self-preservation. But when the moment of destiny came Judas saw that Jesus was going to accept arrest and death and he knew that his plan had gone very wrong, and he went out and flung the money back at the priests and went away and committed suicide. It is likely that Judas tried to make Jesus act and failed, and took his own life when he saw that he had failed.

13

We've got to try to understand why **Judas Iscariot** betrayed **Jesus.** "Iscariot" can be a form of the Latin word "Sicarius" which means a "dagger-bearer"

There was, then, in Palestine a band of men who were the dagger-bearers. They were out to kill every Roman. The dagger-bearers were the most violent **nationalists** of their day

Here we may have the explanation of **Judas.** He was a nationalist

© 1977 WILLIAM BARCLAY & IAIN REID

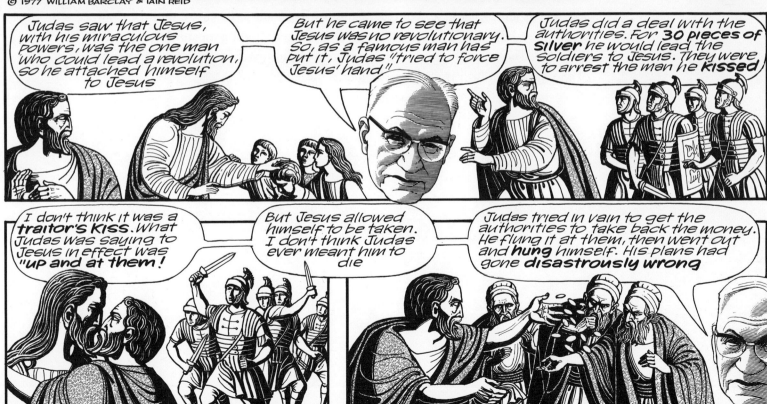

Judas saw that Jesus, with his miraculous powers, was the one man who could lead a revolution, so he attached himself to Jesus

But he came to see that Jesus was no revolutionary. So, as a famous man has put it, Judas "tried to force Jesus' hand."

Judas did a deal with the authorities. For **30 pieces of silver** he would lead the soldiers to Jesus. They were to arrest the man he **kissed**

I don't think it was a **traitor's kiss.** What Judas was saying to Jesus in effect was "**up and at them!**

But Jesus allowed himself to be taken. I don't think Judas ever meant him to die

Judas tried in vain to get the authorities to take back the money. He flung it at them, then went out and **hung** himself. His plans had gone **disastrously wrong**

14

WHAT IS
A PARABLE?

The word 'parable' comes from two Greek words—*para* and *ballein*—which mean to throw or place something alongside something else. So a parable is something placed alongside something else. A parable is usually a story of something that happened on earth which is illustrative of a spiritual or heavenly truth. To put it briefly, a parable is a way of getting from the here and now to the there and then.

There is one special thing to be noticed about the parables of Jesus. They were delivered as open-air preaching and they were delivered to be heard and not to be read. That means that a parable has only one point and it is the point which would strike you whenever you heard it. A parable is not to be studied as if it had been written in a study and was meant for close and detailed study. It is meant to be heard and the point of it is meant to stand out. This means that we do not need to get a meaning for every detail in a parable. The only thing we need to get is the meaning which stands out in the punchline of the parable, which is usually the line at the end.

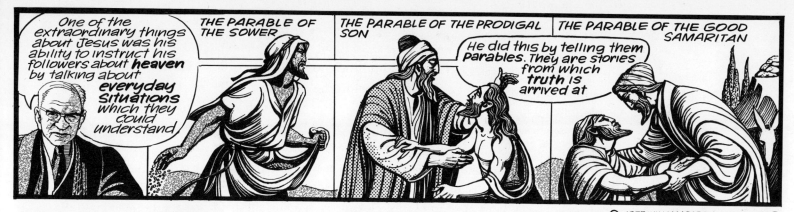

15

THE SOWER

We will now apply what we have learned about the parable to a parable which Jesus told, the parable of the sower. This tells us how a sower went out to sow. The first thing to note is that in Palestine the farmer sowed before he ploughed. He sowed the seed and then ploughed it in. The common ground in Palestine was divided into long narrow strips, and the space between the strips was common ground in a right of way and therefore became beaten as hard as a road by the feet of people continually using it. Some of the seed fell on that kind of path and was not able to penetrate the ground. Some fell on stony ground. The stony ground was not ground full of stones. It was a thin skin of earth over a shelf of rock. In that kind of ground there was no depth and the plant sprang up quickly, only to die from lack of food and moisture. The third kind of ground was ground full of thorns, that is to say, full of fibrous rooted weeds. No doubt they could not be seen but they were there below the ground ready to choke the life out of the seed. The fourth kind of ground was good ground into which the seed fell and brought forth an abundant harvest.

Now let us apply the principle of a parable to that parable. The punchline is the end. It is being heard, therefore there will be one thing which strikes the hearer. The one thing that strikes the hearer is this, that though some of the seed is lost the harvest is sure, and that no farmer will refuse to sow because he knows that some of the seed will inevitably be lost. The meaning of this parable is to teach the disciples, who were growing discouraged, that, in spite of setbacks and in spite of apparent failure, the harvest is sure.

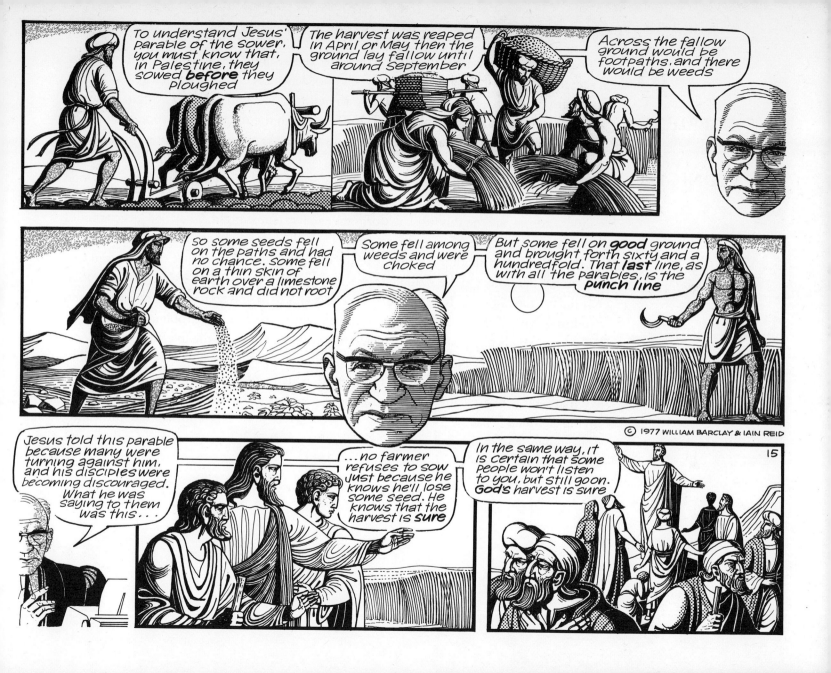

15

16

THE FRIEND AT MIDNIGHT

This parable tells how a visitor came to a home late at night. Hospitality in Palestine was a sacred duty, but the man in the house did not have any food to set before his visitor, so he got up and went to a friend's house to get it. The friend's door was shut. That was a sign that he did not want any visitors. In Palestine in the morning the door was opened and anyone could go out and in. When a door was shut it was a sign that no one was welcome. But the man knocked at the door and kept on knocking. We have to see what the house was like inside. The house was very small and very dark, containing only one room. Two-thirds of it was on ground level, and the third furthest from the door was like a little platform, and on this little platform the family slept at night. They had large families in Palestine, six or seven, or even a dozen. They all slept round the stove, the daughters on the side of their mother with their heads towards her and their feet radiating out like the spokes of a wheel to the wall, and the sons similarly on the father's side. Not only that, but during the night the livestock and the cocks and hens and so forth were brought into the lower part of the house. So to get up at night presented the problem that it would waken everybody else and then you had to find your way through the livestock to the door. The householder did not want to get up, but the man with the visitor knocked so hard that in the end he did get up. This is a parable which works on contrast and it does not say that God is like an unwilling householder who has to be persuaded and cajoled into giving a friend what he needs. What it does say is that, if a churlish and unwilling householder will in the end give a man what he needs, *how much more* will God give his good gifts to those who ask him.

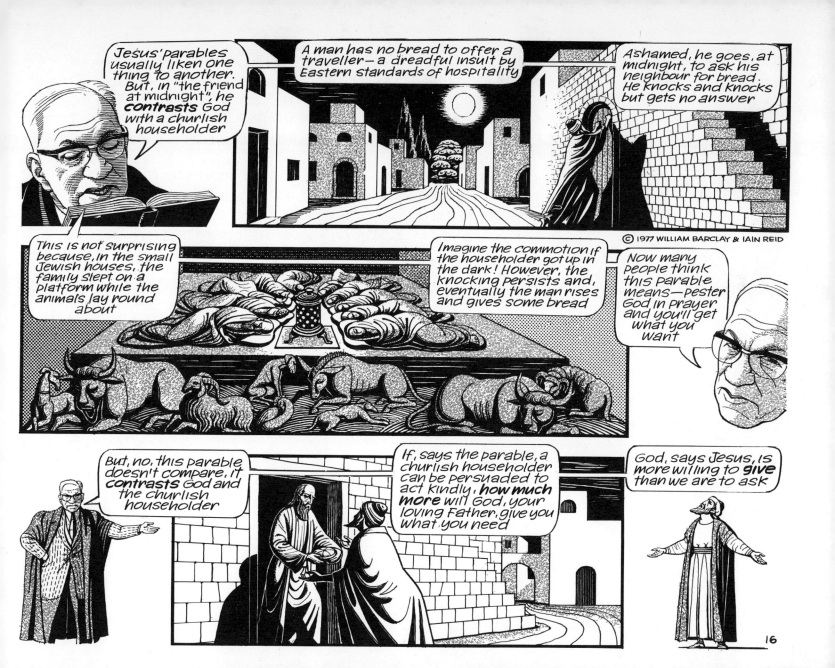

Jesus' parables usually liken one thing to another. But, in "the friend at midnight", he **contrasts** God with a churlish householder

A man has no bread to offer a traveller—a dreadful insult by Eastern standards of hospitality

Ashamed, he goes, at midnight, to ask his neighbour for bread. He knocks and knocks but gets no answer

© 1977 WILLIAM BARCLAY & IAIN REID

This is not surprising because, in the small Jewish houses, the family slept on a platform while the animals lay round about

Imagine the commotion if the householder got up in the dark! However, the knocking persists and, eventually the man rises and gives some bread

Now many people think this parable means—pester God in prayer and you'll get what you want

But, no, this parable doesn't compare, it **contrasts** God and the churlish householder

If, says the parable, a churlish householder can be persuaded to act kindly, **how much more** will God, your loving Father, give you what you need

God, says Jesus, is **more** willing to **give** than we are to ask

16

17

THE UNJUST STEWARD

This is the story of a steward who had been found out in dishonest practices. He knew that his master was about to sack him and he had not the strength to dig and he did not have the nerve to beg. So what was left for him to do? He went round the people who owed things to his master and he said to a man who owed him one hundred measures of oil, write fifty, and to a man who owed him one hundred measures of wheat, write eighty, and when the master found it out he was amused that the steward had been clever enough to make arrangement for his own comfort after he had been sacked.

The point of this parable is that the sons of this world are shrewder in their dealing with their own generation than the sons of light. In other words, if people were as concerned with their Christian life as they are with their comfort, how much better Christians they would be. Worldly men will go to almost any lengths to keep their comfort. The Christian should be just as eager to walk the Christian way.

In Eastern countries, a **steward** had full control of his master's household expenses. Jesus told a parable about a steward who was sacked for lining his own pockets

I'M NOT STRONG ENOUGH TO **DIG** AND I HAVEN'T THE NECK TO **BEG**. I DON'T KNOW WHAT I'M TO DO

17

Then the steward had an idea whereby he would procure the support of his master's **debtors** and put them in a POSITION where he could blackmail them and force them to help him

WHAT DO YOU OWE MY MASTER?

I OWE HIM **100** MEASURES OF OIL

TAKE YOUR BILL, SCORE IT OUT AND WRITE **50!**

He repeated the swindle with a man who owed 100 measures of wheat. Now he had two men who could not give evidence against him for fear of incriminating themselves

IN THEIR DAY AND GENERATION THE CHILDREN OF DARKNESS ARE WISER THAN THE CHILDREN OF LIGHT. THE SONS OF THIS WORLD ARE MORE SHREWD IN DEALING WITH THEIR OWN GENERATION THAN THE SONS OF LIGHT

Jesus was saying that, if the Christian was as earnest about his **Christianity** as the worldly man is about making **money**, he would be a very much better Christian

18

THE WOMAN TAKEN IN ADULTERY

The scribes and Pharisees who brought the woman to Jesus were confronting him with a very real problem, because the penalty for adultery was death (Leviticus 20.10 and Deuteronomy 22.13–24), and death by stoning. So they were indeed confronting Jesus with a problem. The story tells us that Jesus stooped and wrote on the ground. He may have been simply doodling on the ground to gain time before he gave his decision. He may have been writing on the ground, as some manuscripts show, as though he had not heard them. He may have deliberately forced the scribes and Pharisees to repeat their charges, so that in repeating them, they might possibly realise some of the sadistic cruelty that lay behind them. By far the most interesting suggestion comes from one of the later manuscripts. The Armenian translates the passage this way: 'He himself, bowing his head, was writing with his finger in the earth to declare their sins and they were seeing their sins on the stones'. The suggestion is that Jesus was writing in the dust the sins of the very men who were accusing the woman. He was confronting those self-confident sadists with a record of their own sin. However that may be, they got their answer. His answer was: 'All right! Stone her! But let the man who is without sin be the first to cast a stone'. The word for without sin may possibly mean not only without sin but even without a sinful desire. Jesus was saying: 'Yes, you may stone her, but only if you have never wanted to do the same thing yourselves'. There was a silence and the accusers drifted away.

It is to be noted that Jesus did not deal with the woman without sternness. His last words to her were, 'Go and sin no more'. Her forgiveness was not intended as a passport to further sin, but as an obligation to purity.

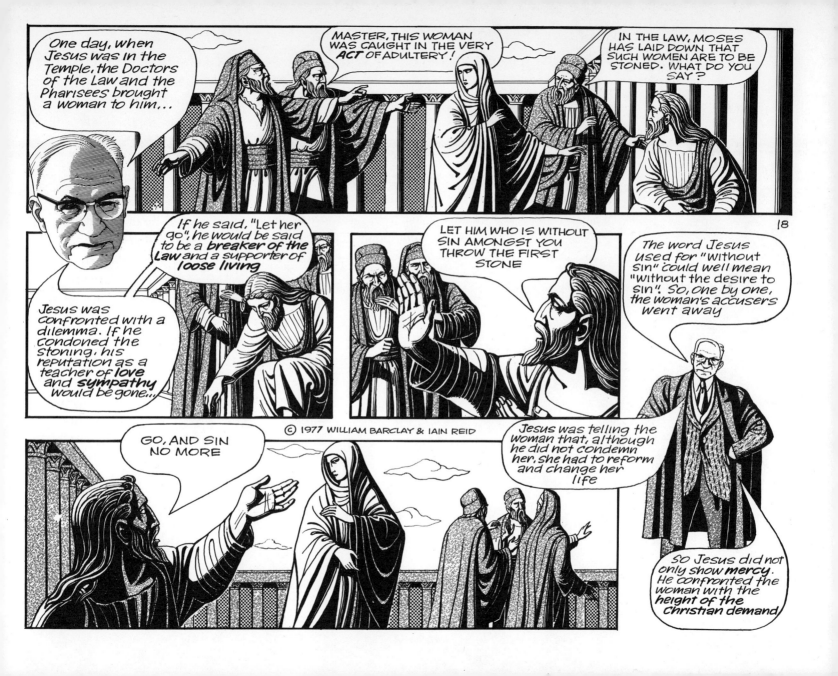

19

THE LOST COIN

Jesus told the story of a woman who lost a silver coin. The floor of a Palestinian house was just beaten earth with dried reeds and rushes on the top of it. The house was very dark because it had only one little window. To search for the coin was much like searching for a needle in a haystack.

It may well be that the coin was doubly precious. A woman in Palestine, before she could be married, had to get herself a necklace made up of ten silver coins, each coin representing a day's wages. This necklace was rather like her wedding ring, and if it was one of the coins meant for that necklace that went lost, then with it there went lost the woman's hopes and dreams of marriage. So she searched until she found it and when at last she found it, she called her neighbours to share in her rejoicing. Jesus told this parable to show that God too knows the joy of finding people who have gone lost.

20

THE GOOD SAMARITAN

Jesus told this story to show who is our neighbour. The road from Jerusalem to Jericho was notoriously dangerous. Jerusalem is 2,300 feet above sea level. The Dead Sea, near which Jericho stood, is 1,300 feet below sea level. The road from Jerusalem to Jericho dropped 3,600 feet in twenty miles. It was therefore a brigands' delight with its narrow rocky defiles and its sudden turns, and even as late as this present century, people had to pay safety money to the sheiks to travel in safety down the road. There are four characters in this parable. There is the traveller, clearly a reckless man because people seldom travelled that road alone, but waited to travel in convoys. There is the priest, who thought that the man was dead and who feared to pollute himself by touching a dead body, and so to lose his turn on priestly duty. There was the Levite, who went over and looked at the man and then passed on. Clearly he was afraid that the man lying at the side of the road was a decoy and that if he stopped to help him the brigands might get him as well. There was the good Samaritan. When Jesus mentioned the Samaritan, people would think the villain was about to arrive, but he was the man who helped the traveller in trouble. So Jesus says your neighbour is anyone in need and you have to help him even if he has nobody but himself to blame for his troubles and even if helping involves some kind of risk.

20

21

THE MAN LET DOWN THROUGH THE ROOF

This is the story of a man whose friends refused to be discouraged. The man was paralysed. They wanted Jesus to cure him but they could not get near Jesus because of the crowd. In Palestine houses were single-room places just like boxes. The roof was made by putting beams across from one wall to another every three or four feet and packing the interval between the beams with dried brushwood and grass and stones lightly cemented together. This meant that you could quite easily take out the material between two beams. This is what these men did. They went up to the roof of the house, removed the material between two beams and let their sick friend down on a stretcher before Jesus. Jesus' first words to the man are, 'Son, your sins are forgiven'. It seems an odd way to start a cure, but in Palestine in the time of Jesus all suffering was traced back to sin. If a man suffered, it meant that he had sinned and this often meant that when a man was suffering, he did come to the conclusion that he had sinned, and of course the more he felt a sinner, the worse his physical condition became. So Jesus began by announcing forgiveness to this man. The orthodox people felt that Jesus had blasphemed by telling the man that he was forgiven. They held that only God could forgive sins, but Jesus put it to them: 'You believe that all suffering is due to sin. This man is cured, therefore you have to believe that his sins have been forgiven'. He caught them out with logical argument.

22

THE GADARENE SWINE

This is the story of how Jesus cured a man who had what the New Testament calls 'an unclean spirit'. In the time of Jesus people believed very definitely in demon possession. These demons were often held to be the spirits of wicked people still carrying on their wickedness after death. The man in this story was a particularly violent case of demon possession. When Jesus asked him his name he said his name was Legion. A Roman Legion had six hundred men in it, so the man must have felt he was possessed by a whole regiment of demons. The man was shouting and shrieking and his shouts and shrieks sent a whole herd of pigs stampeding down the cliffs into the lake. It is highly likely that Jesus used this stampede to say to the man: 'Look, your demons have gone into the pigs and are drowned'. Only by some kind of demonstration could this man have been convinced that he really was cured.

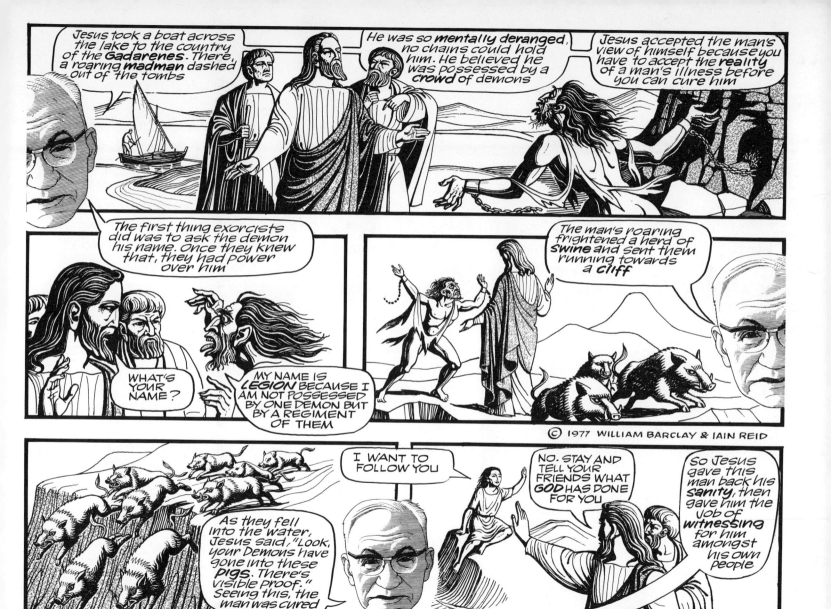

23

THE PHARISEES

'The Pharisees' literally means 'the separated ones'. The Pharisees were the fine flower of Jewish piety, men who had separated themselves from the activities of the world to concentrate on keeping the Law.

The Law had originally been the great principles of the Ten Commandments, but the Jews believed that the Law was perfect and that it therefore must contain explicitly or implicitly a rule and a regulation for every possible man in every possible circumstance in life. They therefore developed a vast edifice known as the oral law or the scribal law, which was just as binding as the original Ten Commandments. For instance, the Ten Commandments bade a man to remember the Sabbath Day to keep it holy and forbade him to work on the Sabbath. The Pharisee was not satisfied with that. He had to define work. So he laid down thirty-nine different fathers of work, thirty-nine different classifications of what constitutes work. One of them was that a burden must not be carried on the Sabbath Day (Jeremiah 17.21). The Pharisee has now to define what is a burden. So he defines a burden as anything which weighs as much as two dried figs. A stone is a burden, but what is a stone? A stone is anything big enough to throw at a bird. So they argued as to whether a man could wear his dentures on the Sabbath, whether he could wear a wooden leg, whether a woman might wear a brooch or false hair, or if these things were carrying burdens. The Pharisees had made of the great principles of the Law a host of little rules and regulations.

One of the things which was work on the Sabbath Day was healing. Nothing could be done to make a man better on a Sabbath Day. Jesus broke this law by healing and encouraged other people to break it by telling them to take up their bed and walk. The bed, of course, was a burden.

To the Pharisees, religion was living life according to these petty rules and regulations. To Jesus, religion was loving God and loving your fellow man. If the Pharisees were right, Jesus was wrong, and if Jesus was right, the Pharisees were wrong. So the Pharisees saw in Jesus a destroyer of all that they reckoned as goodness and were therefore determined to eliminate him.

23

24

YOU ARE THE CHRIST

This episode comes right in the middle of Mark's Gospel, and it is the turning point in the Gospel. The essence of the episode is that Jesus, before he set out on the way to Jerusalem and certainly to die, wanted to be sure that someone knew who he was. So he asked his disciples, 'Who do men say that I am?' And then he asked them the further question 'Who do you say that I am?' Peter answers that he is the Christ, the Son of the Living God.

The scene where this happened is very important. It happened near Caesarea Philippi. Caesarea Philippi had two ancient names. It was called Balinas because it was associated with the worship of Baal. There were no fewer than fourteen pagan temples round about it. It was called Panias because there was a grotto there which was said to be the birthplace of Pan, the Greek God of Nature and, above all, by the time of Jesus, a great shining white temple was erected on a hillside to the godhead of Caesar, and in it the Roman Emperor was worshipped as a God.

It is an intensely dramatic thing for a homeless, penniless Jewish carpenter to ask who men believed him to be and expect the highest answer in the presence of ancient Palestinian religion, in the presence of Greek religion, in the presence of Emperor worship. Jesus in this episode challenges all other ideas of religion in order to make sure that someone gives him the highest place before he sets out to die.

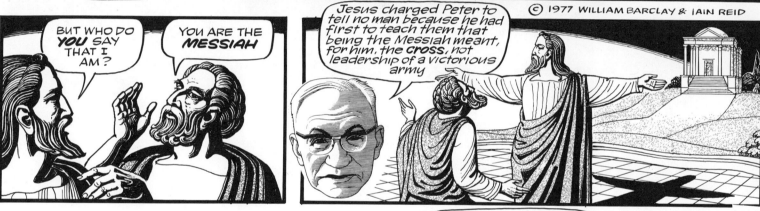

24

25

THE TRANS-FIGURATION

At Caesarea Philippi Jesus attempted and succeeded in getting the approval of men. On the Mount of Transfiguration he gets the divine approval. In the vision which appeared, two men appeared, Elijah and Moses. In these two lay the very essence of Jewish religion. Elijah was the greatest of the prophets and Moses was the supreme law-giver, and these two assured Jesus that he was on the right road, that he should go on, and not only did they assure him, but the voice of God came out of the cloud giving Jesus the divine approval.

If Jesus was to go to Jerusalem in the certainty that he must die, he had to be very sure that he was right. Caesarea Philippi gave him the recognition of men, the Mount of Transfiguration gave him the recognition of the greatest figures of the past and of God himself.

26

WOULD-BE FOLLOWERS

This incident, as it is told to us in Luke 9.57–62, tells how Jesus dealt with three would-be followers. To the first man he says that foxes have holes and the birds of the air have nests but he has nowhere to lay his head. In other words, he says to the man: 'Before you think of following me count the cost, reckon up just what following me involves'. Jesus was completely honest and would have no man under false pretences. The second man says that he will follow Jesus, but let him first go and bury his father, and Jesus tells him to let the dead bury their dead, but to come to follow him there and then. This is not so hard as it appears to be. For what the man probably said was that he would follow Jesus after his father had died. We are told of the case of a brilliant young Arab who was given the chance to study at Oxford or Cambridge and who said he would come when he had buried his father. His father at the time was little more than forty and what the young man meant was that he would stay where he was until his father had died. Jesus says that that is wrong, that the impulse to follow him must be obeyed at once or it may never come back. The third person wants to go home and say goodbye to the people in his house. Jesus' answer to him is that no man who puts his hand to the plough can look back and drive a straight furrow. This means that when a man follows Jesus he must have no regretful backward looks at the kind of life he used to live and the kind of people he used to know. His look must always be forward.

This is the story of three would-be followers of Jesus. The first man came and said, "I will follow you wherever you go"

FOXES HAVE HOLES AND BIRDS HAVE NESTS, BUT THE SON OF MAN HAS NOWHERE TO LAY HIS HEAD

Jesus was warning the man of the life he would have to live. Only if he had the stomach for it should he become a follower

26

Another man came and Jesus said, "Follow me." The man replied, "Let me first go and bury my father."

LET THE DEAD BURY THE DEAD

This sounds harsh to modern ears. But Jesus was simply telling the man to make up his mind. You see, the man did not mean that his father was dead

The man was playing for time. He wanted to **wait** until his father died before he followed Jesus. It could mean a wait of 20 or 30 years

A third said, "I will follow you, but first let me go and say goodbye to those who are at home." Jesus said a thing that a Ploughman knows is true...

NO PLOUGHMAN CAN PLOUGH A STRAIGHT FURROW LOOKING BACK. IF YOU PUT YOUR HAND TO THE PLOUGH YOU'VE GOT TO COME STRAIGHT FOR THE KINGDOM OF GOD

This was Jesus demanding **complete decision**, not a looking-back decision, but a decision that looks only forward to the life that he will live

27

THE RICH YOUNG RULER

This episode tells how a rich young man came to Jesus and asked what he must do to inherit eternal life. Jesus told him to keep the commandments and he said he had kept them all. Now, there is another version of this story which is in the Gospel according to the Hebrews, a gospel which did not get into the New Testament, and it has some very valuable additional explanation. Jesus said to the man: 'Fulfil the law of the prophets'. He answers him: 'I have kept them'. Jesus said: 'Go, sell all that you have and distribute it to the poor, and come and follow me.' The rich man was obviously unwilling to do this and Jesus said to him: 'How can you say, "I have kept the law of the prophets", for it is written in the law that you must love your neighbour as yourself, and many of your brothers, sons of Abraham, are clad in filth and dying of hunger, and your house is full of good things and nothing at all goes out to them'. The point about this is that the young man did not really keep the commandments at all, and the thing that kept him from obeying the commandments was that he was too attached to his wealth to be able to be generous with it. This is not a commandment from Jesus to every man. It is only a commandment to the man who has become shackled by his wealth, and who is mastered by his wealth rather than master of it.

28

JAMES AND JOHN

The disciples never to the end of the day managed to get rid of the standard Jewish idea of the Messiah. To them the Messiah was to be a great figure of world conquest, and that is the career they looked to Jesus to begin, and when he was on his way to Jerusalem, James and John tried to steal a march on their fellow disciples by asking Jesus to give them the principal places when he came into his kingdom. This is usually taken as a proof of the utter worldly-mindedness of James and John, but it is a proof of more than that. It is a proof of the most extraordinary faith. Jesus was on his way to Jerusalem. In Jerusalem he would most certainly die, and yet these two disciples of his were perfectly confident that in the end he would emerge victorious. The incident is not so much a condemnation of the ambition of James and John as it is a commendation of their extraordinary faith in Jesus.

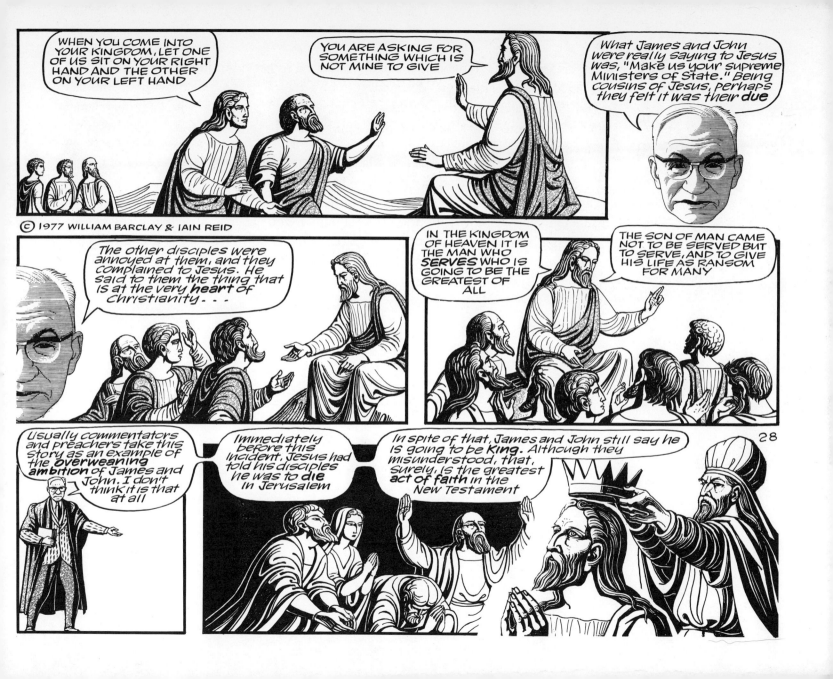

28

29

JESUS AND THE CHILDREN

The story of the children being brought to Jesus is a natural story. It was natural for mothers to want their boys and girls to be touched by the hand of a holy man, and that is what was happening when they tried to bring their children to Jesus. On the other hand, it was also natural for the disciples to try to protect Jesus. Jesus was on the way to Jerusalem to die. We read of the atmosphere of the time in Mark, chapter 10, verses 31–34. The tension and the terror are painted there. So what the disciples felt was that they could not think that Jesus could be bothered with children at a time like that in his life. But there was no time when Jesus was too busy for the child. For the child has at least three things which make him typical of the entrant to the kingdom of God. There is the child's trust. There is the child's wonder at the world. And there is the child's forgiveness. There is all the difference in the world between being childish and childlike, and it is the childlike spirit which is equipped to enter the kingdom.

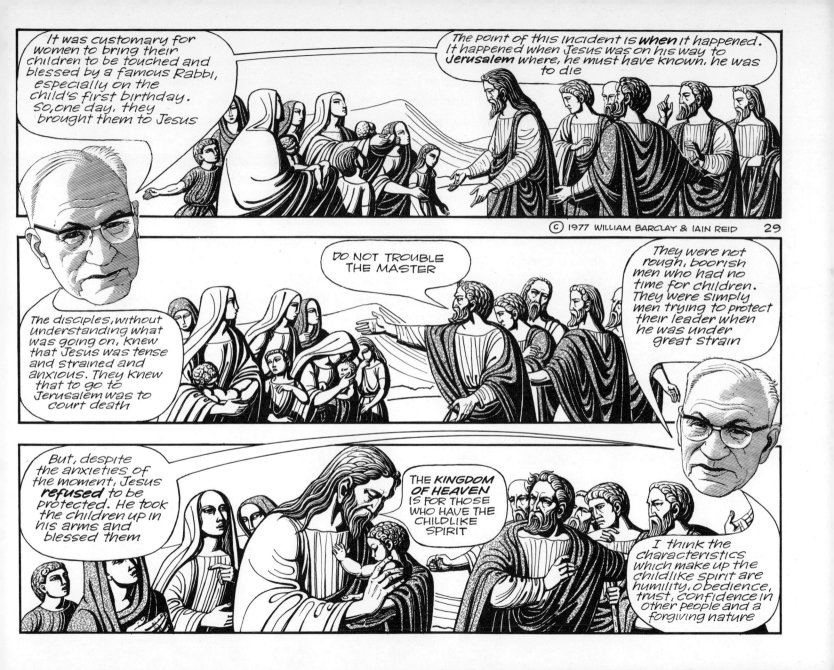

30

ZACCHAEUS

This incident happened near Jericho. Jericho was a very wealthy and very beautiful city. It commanded a main road to Jerusalem and it also commanded the main roads across the Jordan to the trans-Jordan lands. It was therefore a place where customs collecting was extremely important. Everyone in Palestine had to pay certain taxes. Everyone had to pay poll tax simply for the privilege of existing. There was a ground tax, which consisted of one-tenth of all the grain grown and one-fifth of the wine and the oil. This could be paid in kind or commuted into money. There was an income tax, which was 1 percent of a man's income. In these taxes there was not a great deal of room for extortion, but there were other kinds of duties. A tax was payable for using the main roads, the harbours, the markets. A tax was payable on a cart, on each wheel of it and on the animal which drew it. There was purchase tax on certain articles and there were import and export duties. Ordinary people had no idea how much they ought to pay, and so the tax collectors could charge them pretty nearly what they liked. That is the kind of person Zacchaeus was. He was a Jew who had sold himself into the hands of his country's enemies to get rich quickly and to get rich easily. He seeks to guarantee his conversion because he says that he is going to give back what he had taken from any man four times over. That had only to be done if there was robbery and the original goods were not restorable, and that had to be robbery with violence. Ordinary robbery, in which the original goods were restorable, was satisfied by repayment of double the value. If voluntary confession was made and voluntary restitution was offered the value of the original goods had to be paid plus one-fifth. It can be seen that Zacchaeus was going to go far beyond what was necessary to prove that he was a changed man.

31

WOMAN OF SAMARIA

Jesus and his disciples had come in their journey to the Well of Sychar near Samaria. The disciples had gone off to get themselves food. When they came back they were shocked and astonished to find Jesus talking to the Samaritan woman. In the first place she was a woman, and no respectable Jewish Rabbi would ever be seen talking to a woman in public, not even to his wife or sister. In the second place, she was a Samaritan, and the Jews had no dealings with the Samaritans. But Jesus spoke to the woman and actually revealed himself to her. She went back to the town and told the others what had happened to her, but the people of Samaria came themselves to see Jesus and believed from their own experience of him and not just from what the woman had told them of him. This is an amazing example of Jesus revealing himself to the most unlikely of persons.

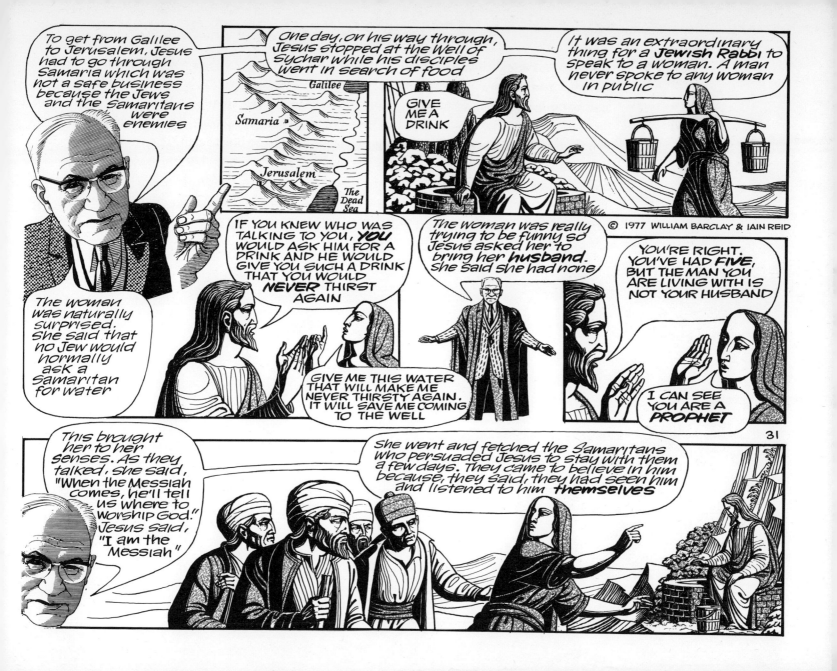

32

NICODEMUS

Nicodemus was a distinguished figure amongst the Jews. He was a member of the Sanhedrin, but what he had heard and seen of Jesus disturbed him deeply. So he came to Jesus, and we note that he came at night. He did not want to be seen coming to Jesus, so he came then, when no one could see him. It is to Nicodemus that Jesus made the great statement that if a man was going to enter the kingdom he needed to be born again. The word 'again' in Greek is *anothen* and it can mean either 'again' or 'from above'. In this case it means both. It means that a man has to be born again from above if he is to enter the kingdom. That is to say that he is to make a complete break with his past and enter on a completely new life.

© 1977 WILLIAM BARCLAY & IAIN REID

33

THE TRIUMPHAL ENTRY

In regard to this incident in the life of Jesus it is important to note three things.

1. What was Jesus doing? It is easy to make a mistake here. It says that he came riding into Jerusalem on an ass. The ass in Palestine was not the humble donkey of the west, the ass was a noble animal and was the animal on which kings rode when they came to their subjects in peace. The horse was the animal of war. So, in the triumphal entry Jesus was claiming to be king, but claiming to be king of peace and not king of war.

2. We must note where he did it. Jesus made this demonstration in the days just preceding the Passover Feast. The numbers who came to the Passover were legion. Some years later, a governor called Cestius took a census of the number of lambs slain at a Passover, and the number came to 236,000. According to Passover regulations, there must be a minimum of ten people to every lamb. Therefore there must have been about 2 1/2 million people in Jerusalem at the Passover time. Although Jesus knew that the authorities were out for his life, he rode into Jerusalem at the busiest time of all and in such a way that it would focus every eye upon himself.

3. We must note what the people said. They shouted their hosanna. Hosanna is really a quotation from Psalm 118.25: 'Save us, we beseech thee, O Lord'. Hosanna is the cry addressed to a king or a person of high degree by people in suffering or distress and means 'save now'. It had perhaps lost its original meaning and was simply used to mean 'hail', just as hallelujah has lost its original meaning and is uttered chiefly as a shout of praise.

The entry is obviously a great proof of the courage of Jesus in that he faced the mob at the certain peril of his life, and it is a great proof of the kind of invitation he was making to them. He wanted them to invite him to be their king, but their king in peace and love.

33

Jesus made his **triumphal entry** into **Jerusalem** a week before the **Passover** which was the greatest feast of the **Jews**

It was the ambition of every Jew to celebrate one **Passover** in the city of **Jerusalem**

Evidence suggests that there were **2½ million** people there that year. Jews had come from literally every nation under the sun

Although Jesus had a price on his head, he did not skulk quietly into the city hoping nobody would notice him

He came riding on an **ass**. Such an entry was bound to focus attention on him

In the ancient world, the ass was a **splendid beast**. When a **king** came in **peace** he rode on an ass. Only in **war** did he ride on a horse

© 1977 WILLIAM BARCLAY & IAIN REID

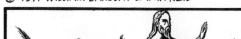

Jesus' triumphal entry therefore was an act of **colossal courage**. He was facing the mob

Also, he was saying, "I am the **Prince of Peace**, I am not coming in war, I am coming in peace and love"

Jesus was making his **last appeal** to the people to **take him for what he is**

34

CLEANSING THE TEMPLE

The Temple in Jerusalem consisted of a series of courts, each rising higher than the one that went before and each one more private than the one that went before. The outermost court was the Court of the Gentiles, into which anyone might go. The next was the Court of the Women, and no Gentile might pass the barrier between it and the Court of the Gentiles, under penalty of death. The next was the Court of the Israelites, and the last was the Court of the Priests, where the great Altar of the Burnt Offering was.

This incident took place in the Court of the Gentiles. Jesus overturned the tables of the money changers. There was a Temple tax to be paid by everyone and it was commonly paid at the time of the Passover season. People brought coinage of all kinds because all kinds of coinage were valid for ordinary everyday purposes. But the Temple tax had to be paid in a currency which did not have a king's head on it because, to the Jew, a coin with a king's head was a graven image. The money changers therefore changed the coins, but they charged each pilgrim the equivalent of two pence for changing the money and they charged them another two pence for giving them their change. The amount this came to can be seen from the fact that four pence was the equivalent of a working man's day's wage. Jesus was infuriated at the ramp that was being carried out on defenceless pilgrims. He also drove out the sellers of doves. Nearly everyone who came to the Temple brought an offering. You could buy doves outside the Temple, but the Temple had appointed Temple inspectors and they would be certain to find a fault or flaw in any animal bought outside. They would say: 'Just buy one from our Temple stalls. They have already been inspected'. The difficulty was that outside a pair of doves might cost as little as four pence, while inside they might cost as much as 180 pence, and the profits went to the family of Annas, for the booths were known as the Bazaars of Annas. Jesus swept the money changers and the cattle dealers out of the Temple because they were turning the only part of it into which the Gentiles could go into a shop, and a dishonest shop at that.

The Temple was composed of a series of courts. The outside court was the **Court of the Gentiles** where anyone could come. Jesus often taught there. Also there were moneychangers and sellers of sacrificial animals

All Jews had to pay a Temple tax of half a shekel, about 25 pence, which was a lot of money. The working man's wage in Palestine was **four pence** a day

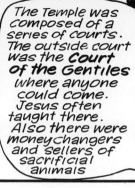

The tax had to be paid either in **Sanctuary Shekels** or **Galilean Half-Shekels** as all other currencies had a king's head on them and were considered to be **graven images**

The moneychangers' charges were **steep**. They even charged for giving a man his **change**! So the poor chap ended up paying about **double**! This racket belonged to **Annas** who was raking in about **£70,000** a year!

There was another racket. When the poor people brought their sacrifices, these had to be inspected

SORRY. IT'S **BLEMISHED**. YOU CAN'T OFFER IT. BUY ONE FROM THE BOOTHS WHERE THE ANIMALS HAVE ALREADY BEEN INSPECTED

34

But there the animals cost **25 times** more than they did outside

So Jesus took a cord of whips and thrashed these people out of the Temple

He did so, I think, for three reasons. One, it was not the kind of thing to do in **God's house**. Two, the **poor** were being fleeced

Three, this was happening in the Court of the Gentiles, so the Gentiles were losing the chance to worship God as they liked

35

THE WICKED HUSBANDMAN

This is an allegory more than it is a parable. The likening of Israel to a vineyard was something they knew well. Isaiah, chapter 5, drew that picture. The story is quite natural. Palestine was not a rich country and not a comfortable country and therefore there were many absentee landlords whose only interest in their estates was to draw the revenue from them when the time came for paying the rent. In this story the owner of the vineyard first sent his servants to collect the rent, and they were shamefully ill-used and maltreated. He finally sent his son, and the husbandmen killed the son hoping that they might inherit the vineyard themselves. The owner of the vineyard took a swift vengeance on them and gave the vineyard to other husbandmen to keep.

The vineyard is Israel, the servants who were sent are the prophets, the son who was sent is Jesus himself, and the story tells us that Jesus knew perfectly well when he went to Jerusalem that he was on the way to die. The parable was a warning, but it was a warning which was not taken.

36

THE ANOINTING AT BETHANY

Jesus was very much at home in the house of Martha and Mary and their brother, Lazarus, in Bethany. When he was there Mary did a very lovely thing to him. Jewish women were very fond of perfume and they wore round their necks a little phial of very precious, very expensive perfume. Some of these phials were said to cost as much as £40. Mary took her phial of perfume and broke it over Jesus to anoint him with it.

Immediately the complaint was made: 'What waste'. But love must always give its very best and love is an extravagant thing rather than a niggardly thing. It was also protested that the money might have been given to the poor, but Jesus answered that if they wanted to help the poor they could do it at any time. If they wanted to do something to tell him how much they loved him, it had to be done there and then because he was on his way to death. This story shows how right it is of love to be extravagant at a time when a gift is possible.

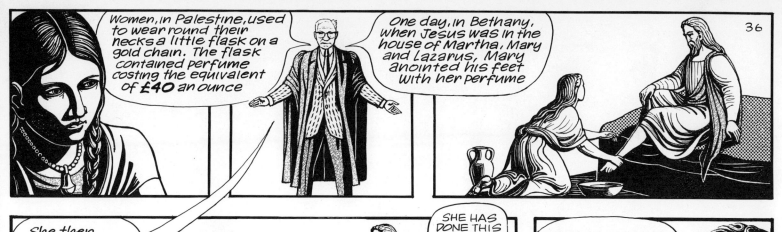

37

THE LAST SUPPER

When the Passover time came round Jesus determined to celebrate the festival with his own men.

The prophets of Israel had a habit which is called dramatic prophetic action. In this, when people would not listen, they did something to make them at least look. For instance, when the prophet Elijah wished to warn Jeroboam that ten of the tribes were going to revolt against him, he met Jeroboam in the street. He slipped out of his robe, tore it into twelve pieces and gave ten of them to Jeroboam, as a sign that the ten tribes were going to rebel. The people might not listen to words, but they would certainly look at this kind of striptease act performed on a public highway.

So Jesus uses dramatic prophetic action at the Last Supper. He took the bread and broke it, he took the wine and poured it out, and said, 'Look, just as this bread is broken, my body is to be broken for you. Just as this scarlet wine is poured out, my blood is to be poured out for you'. It was a demonstration of what was going to happen. And this is the memorial festival which the church has kept and in which it has met Jesus again from that day to this.

38

THE FOOT WASHING

The roads in Palestine were what we would call unsurfaced roads. They were therefore thick with dust. The shoes that the Palestinians wore were sandals with no socks or stockings, and therefore the feet became very dusty if any distance was walked. For that reason, if anyone was holding a party, there was a slave at the door with water to wash guests' feet before they sat at table. Of course, when Jesus and the twelve came to sit at their meal there was no slave and there was none of them willing to undertake a slave's duty, so Jesus did it himself. He girded himself with a towel and he took a basin and a ewer of water and washed his disciples' feet. The washing was done by pouring fresh water over the feet. The Palestinians would have thought it an incredibly dirty habit to use the same water to wash two people's feet, so they poured the water from a kind of ewer over the feet into a basin and washed the feet that way. Jesus, on this occasion, was giving his disciples another lesson in action. He was telling them that if he, their master, was willing to wash their feet, they too ought to have the humility which would accept the humblest duties, that is, a humility born of love.

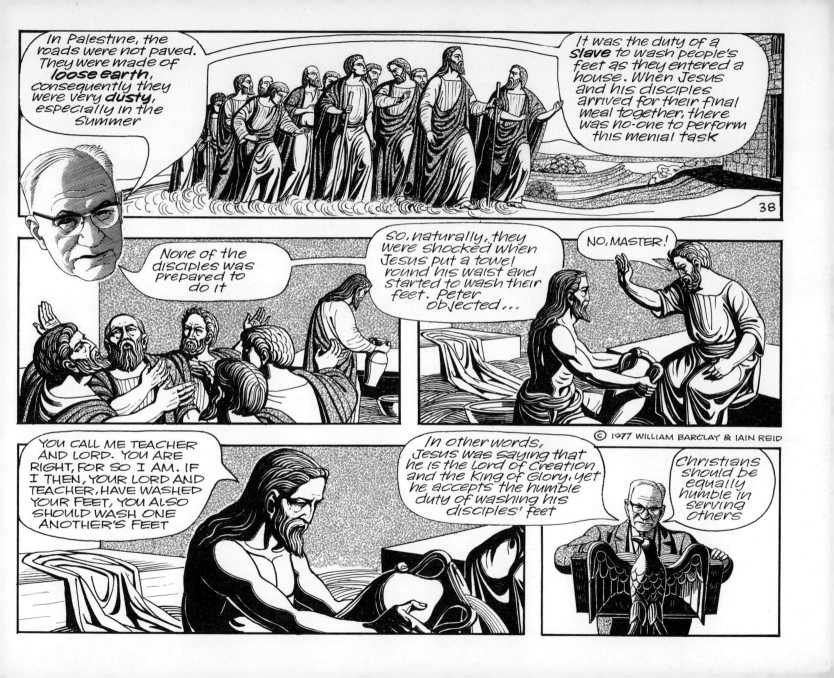

39

GETHSEMANE

One of the interesting things about the last days of Jesus' life is the number of unknown and un-named people who did things for him. Someone gave him the colt on which he rode into Jerusalem. Someone gave him the upper room where the Last Supper was held, and now someone must have given him the Garden of Gethsemane. There are few or no gardens in Jerusalem because there is so little space, Jerusalem being built on the top of a hill, and only the well-to-do had private gardens on the Mount of Olives, and it was no doubt into one of these private gardens that Jesus was given access by an unknown friend.

He went there to fight his last battle with himself. He took the three disciples with him, Peter, James and John, but they were so exhausted physically and mentally that they were unable to stay awake while he prayed. He prayed that this cup might be taken from him. The prayer was not answered that way, but it was answered by the fact that he received the strength and courage to go through his terrible ordeal. Gethsemane is not a case of unanswered prayer. It is the final proof that prayer is not a means of escape, but a means of victory.

There were, for two reasons, no **gardens** in the city of Jerusalem...

One, there wasn't any **room**, the city being built on top of a hill. Two, it would have been considered **blasphemous** to put **manure** on the ground of the Holy City

But wealthy persons had gardens on the **Mount of Olives**, just outside the city

39

The disciples were so emotionally and physically exhausted they could not stay awake which must have been rather terrible for Jesus. In his biggest hour of trial, his friends couldn't help him

Some unknown friend must have given Jesus permission to use his garden in Gethsemane. After the **Last Supper**, Jesus went there with Peter, James and John

IF IT BE POSSIBLE, TAKE THIS DREADFUL EXPERIENCE AWAY FROM ME. BUT NOT WHAT **I** WANT— WHAT **YOU** WANT

Three times Jesus prayed that prayer. No-one wants to die at **33**, and no-one wants to die on a **cross** at any age

I have previously said that Jesus' essential message was the kingdom of God, and that the essential meaning of the kingdom of God is **to do God's will**

Jesus' prayer showed that he was ready to do the will of God even if it meant his **death**

At that moment, the Jews arrived. They had gone to the Romans and had got themselves soldiers to arrest Jesus and take him away

40

TRIAL NO. 1

Jesus underwent two trials at least on the night before his crucifixion. His appearance before the Sanhedrin was not so much a trial as an investigation. If it had been a trial, it would have been illegal. The Sanhedrin could not meet at night. When it met, every individual had to give his verdict separately, beginning from the youngest to the oldest. If the decision was the death penalty, it could not be imposed on the same day. There must be another night between the verdict and the execution, in order to give the judges time to sleep on their decision and possibly to change their minds. Regarded as a trial, the trial of Jesus before the Jews was rather a lynching, but it probably was not meant to be a trial. It was an investigation to find a charge.

40

41

TRIAL NO. 2

The charge which the Jews extracted at their own investigation was that Jesus claimed to be the Son of God, the Messiah, but that was not the charge on which they brought him before Pilate. They brought him before Pilate on the ground that he was setting himself up as king in opposition to Caesar, which they knew was not true.

The trial before Pilate was a Roman trial. The Jews, being a subject people, had not the right to execute anyone without the consent of the the Romans, and that is why Jesus had to be tried before Pilate as well as before the Sanhedrin. It is abundantly clear that Pilate did not want to crucify Jesus. He was in fact blackmailed into doing it.

When Roman Governors marched into Jerusalem they had, up until Pilate, dismantled their regimental standards. The standards were not flags. They were poles with a little image of the Emperor at the end of them—therefore a graven image. Pilate refused to do this. The people sent a deputation to him. He would not listen to them. At last he told them to meet him in a wide open space and surrounded them with his soldiers and informed them that unless they stopped their requests he would order the soldiers to fall on them and cut them to death. The people said they would rather die than have these defiled standards in their city, and Pilate had to give in. Pilate did another foolish thing. He wanted to bring a fresh water supply into Jerusalem. The water supply was poor in the city. He took money from the Temple treasury to build an aqueduct, and the fact that he had raided the treasury produced riots. He put his soldiers in plain clothes amongst the crowds and then went and appealed to the crowds to disband. They did not do so. The soldiers were ordered to fall on them with clubs and they got out of hand a bit and people were killed in the riot. Now subject provinces had the right to report their Governor to headquarters in Rome if he exceeded his rights, and the Jews said to Pilate: 'If you let this man go, you are not Caesar's friend'. In other words, they said: 'Do what we want you to do or we will report you'. Pilate's past blackmailed him into crucifying Jesus. Jesus got no justice at the time of his trial.

42

THE CROSS

The cross was a punishment that was kept for slaves and foreigners. It would have been illegal to crucify a Roman citizen. When the verdict was passed, the crosspiece of the cross was laid on the shoulders of the criminal. He was then taken by the longest possible route to the place of crucifixion in order that as many people as possible should see what happened to the law-breaker. When they arrived at the place of crucifixion, the cross was laid flat on the ground. The criminal was stretched upon it. His hands were nailed to the cross. Commonly his feet were only loosely bound. There was a piece of wood which projected from the cross between the prisoner's legs which supported his weight or his hands would have been torn in pieces. Normally prisoners were given a narcotic drug to ease the pain, but Jesus refused to take the drug. He would meet death open-eyed and at its worst. Crucifixion did not necessarily kill a man, and once a man was nailed to the cross he was left to die. Jesus died mercifully quickly, for sometimes a man could hang on the cross for a week until he died, maddened by pain and thirst.

43

THE RESURREC-TION 1

The Resurrection is the supreme miracle of the Gospels. It is not strange that people have tried to find grounds to disbelieve in it. It has been argued that Jesus did not die on the cross, that he only fainted and revived in the cool of the tomb and rid himself of the grave clothes, and so escaped. It has been argued that the disciples took his body away and then said that he had risen from the dead. It has been argued that the Jews took his body away in order to prevent his tomb becoming a place of pilgrimage for his followers and to prevent him becoming a martyr. None of these arguments against the Resurrection will hold water.

44

THE RESURREC-TION 2

One thing stands out about the Resurrection stories. The appearances of Jesus were always to people who loved him and who were thinking of their love. He appeared to Peter in Peter's heart-broken love after his denial of his Lord. He appeared to Mary who loved him more than any other human being. He appeared to the ten and eleven disciples when they were talking of him and thinking of him. He appeared on the road to Emmaus to those who were remembering him and who were regretting his passing. Always, Jesus appeared to those who loved him.

© 1977 WILLIAM BARCLAY & IAIN REID

44

45

THE ROAD TO EMMAUS

When Jesus rose from the dead, he clearly had some special kind of body, because he could come and go at will. When he was with the two in the village house at Emmaus he vanished out of their sight after the meal. When the ten—for Thomas was not there—were meeting in the upper room, it says that suddenly he was in the midst of them. He was apparently independent of space and time and could go when and where he wanted. Another thing to notice is that he apparently appeared only to those who loved him. If we were writing a life of Jesus and trying to make it fictionally exciting, when he rose from the dead we would have him appear to Pilate and to Caiaphas and say to them triumphantly: 'I'm back. What are you going to do about it?' But that is not what he did. He appeared only to people who loved him, who were talking about him and who were longing for him. We talk about the Risen Christ and we talk about it still being possible to meet him. It is quite certain that if we loved him more we would meet him more.

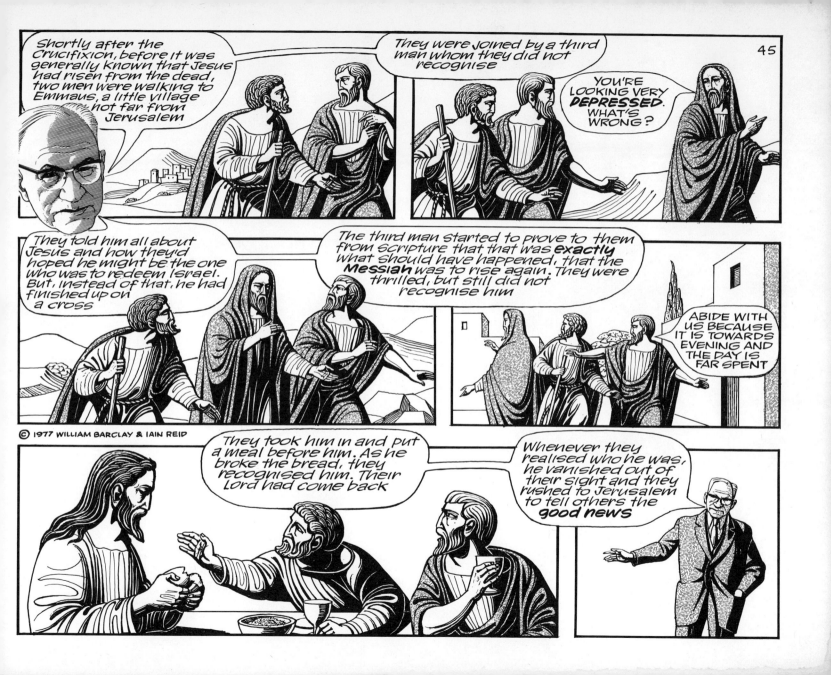